Buddy Bee's Underwater Friends

Written and illustrated by Greg Armstrong

© 2013 Buddy's World and Friends. All rights reserved.

www.buddysworldandfriends.com

On a warm sunny day, Buddy meets with some of his friends for an ocean adventure.

"What is that, Buddy?" his friends ask.
"It's called the Buddy Sub, and it's going to take us to meet some new friends," Buddy replies.

"Where are you taking us to meet our new friends?" they ask.

Buddy says, "All of our new friends live in the ocean and are very excited to meet you."

When everyone was safely on board, Buddy shouted, "Dive! Dive! Dive!"

The submarine starts to go deeper and deeper into the ocean.

As they get deeper, they see many different kinds of sea life. The ocean is full of life!

The first friend they meet is a seal. He greets his new friends by playing and doing flips for them.

As fast as the seals appeared they were gone. What made them swim away so fast? Oh no, sharks.

Buddy tells his friends to keep looking. When suddenly, a group of dolphins start to play.

Soon the dolphins
finished playing.
Schnoodle said,
"I thought horses
lived on a farm." Buddy
replied, "They do. That
is called a seahorse."

"Buddy, those fish look like they're flying in the water!"
Buddy replies, "Those are called stingrays and they glide through the water."

Some of the sea friends are very helpful. Like the sea turtle, who helps a crab by giving him a ride home.

Buddy says, "Did you know that fish go to school?
Just kidding. When fish swim together it's called a SCHOOL."

Then Buddy says, "There is a Pufferfish. When he is afraid, he puffs up. But it's okay, we are his friends."

"Wow, what is that?
You can see right
through it, and it has
such pretty colors!"
Buddy says,
"It's called a Jellyfish."

Suddenly, it got dark.
Buddy said,
"Our largest friend
has come to visit.
It's a whale!"

"Some of our friends live on the ocean floor, or hide in rocks. Like our friend the Octopus."

"Another one of our friends who lives on the bottom is the giant clam. He traps his food when he opens his shell."

The Starfish live on the corals and help keep them clean by removing algae.

Buddy's friends shout, "Be careful Buddy, that crab is going to get us!" "It's okay." Buddy says, "They only grab fish, and he's showing you his catch."

"Buddy, why is that fish inside a plant?"
Buddy replies, "That is a sea anemone, and the fish is feeding it. The anemone also provides a home for the Clownfish."

Did you know that some ocean animals carry their home on their backs? Look at the Hermit Crab.

Is this a forest in the ocean? Buddy says, "It's called a kelp bed. Kelp makes oxygen for all the fish. It also protects the small animals from the big ones."

"Surface! Surface!" Buddy shouts. "Look, we are getting a great send-off by some of our new friends!"

Nosey runs to the end of the pier to greet them and to hear about their underwater adventure. Moments later, the submarine comes to the surface.

As the submarine comes to rest, they are all greeted by some of their new sea friends!

Buddy has a surprise for everyone. He gives them each a captains' hat for their first adventure at sea.

Thank you for taking the underwater adventure with us! We hope that you enjoyed meeting our new sea friends. See you next time!

Please take care of our new friends by taking care of our oceans.

Captain Buddy

www.ingramcontent.com/pod-product-compliance
Lightning Source LLC
Chambersburg PA
CBHW041950110426
42744CB00026B/6